colors abc numbers

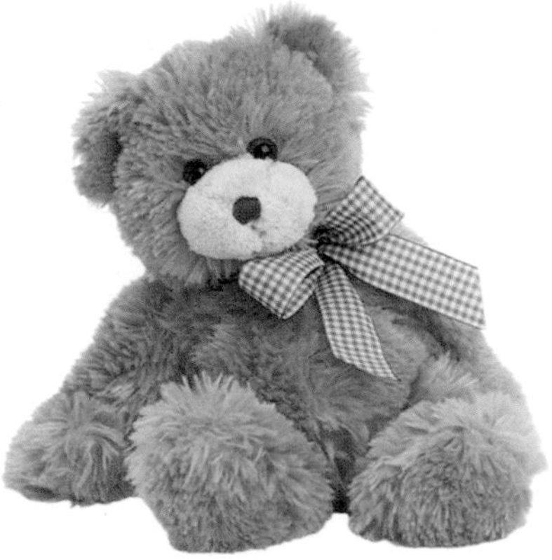
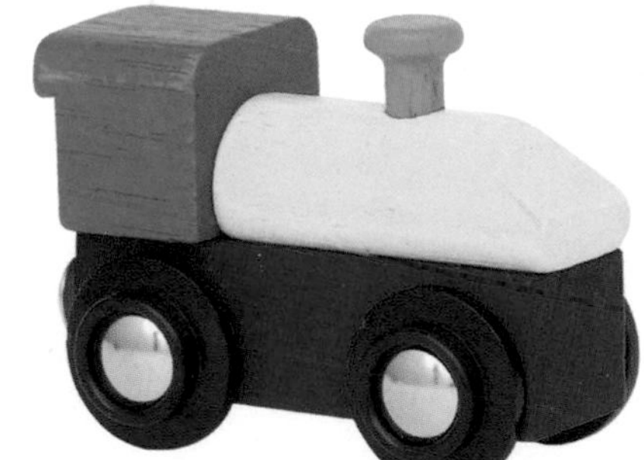
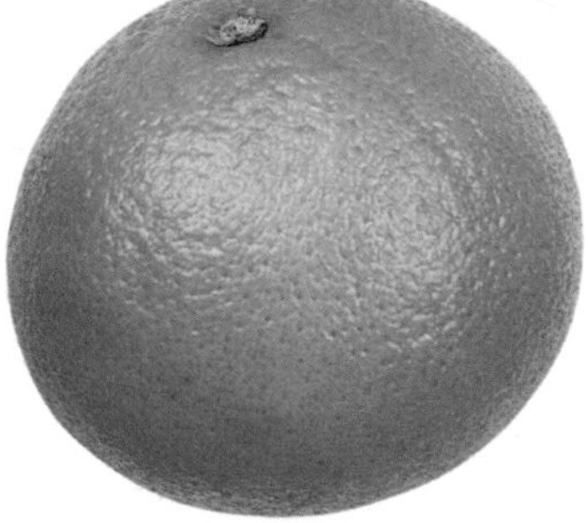

priddy books

First words

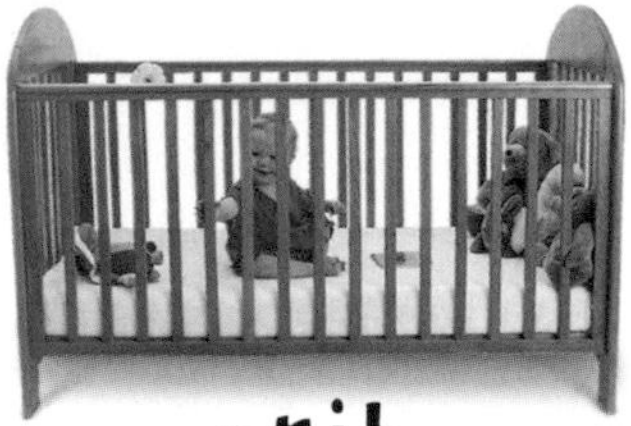

crib

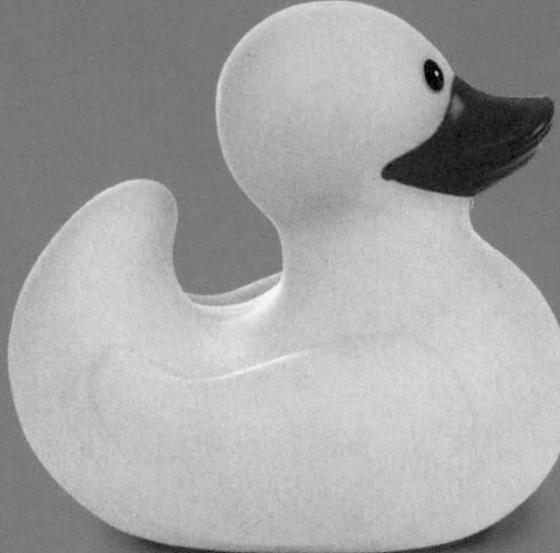

duck

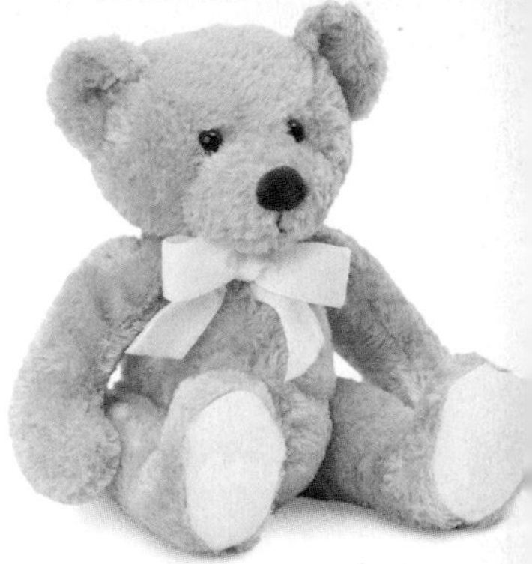

teddy bear

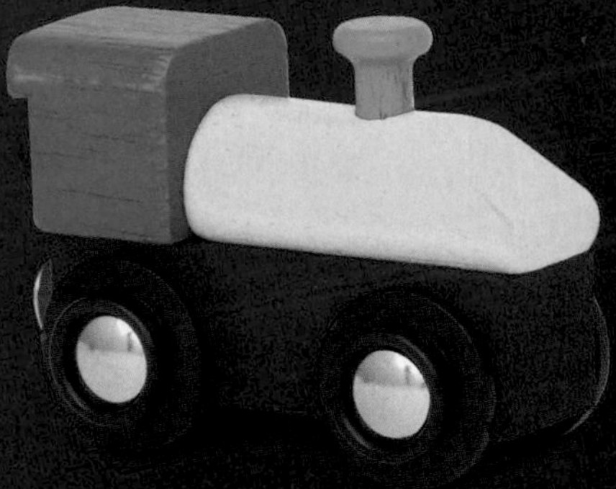

flower

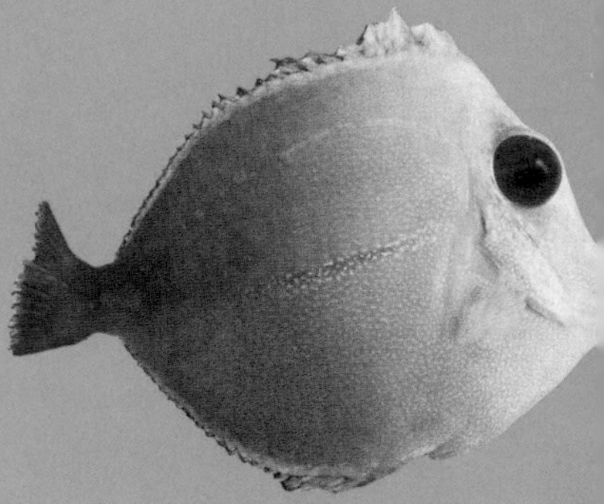

fish

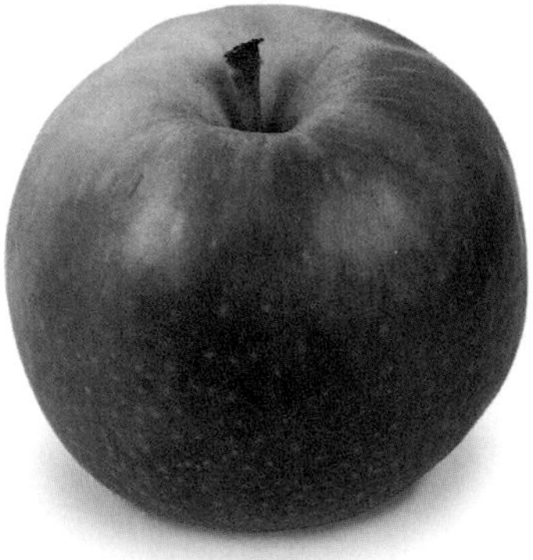

apple

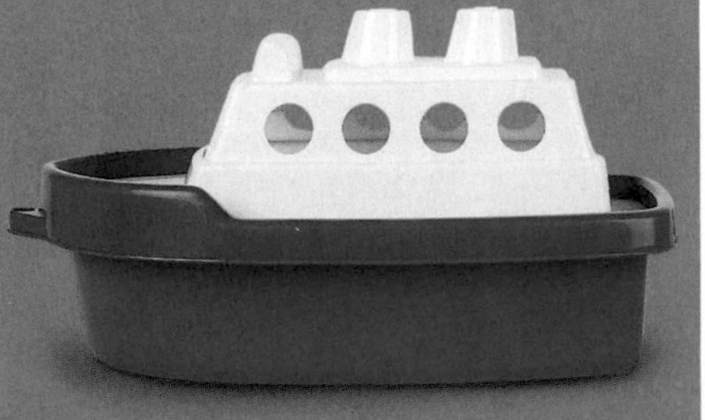

boat

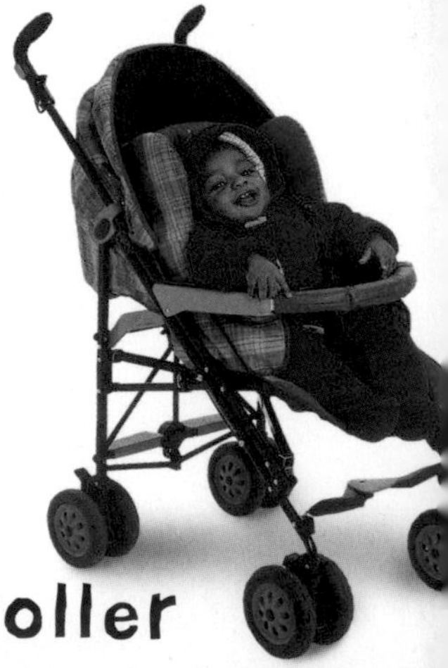

stroller